What Is a Christian?

Answers for Kids

Lifeway Press®
Brentwood, TN 37027

EDITORIAL TEAM
KIDS MINISTRY PUBLISHING

Chuck Peters
Director, Lifeway NextGen

Jeremy Carroll
Publishing Manager,
VBS, Hyfi, and Kids Discipleship

Kayla Stevens
Publishing Team Leader
and Content Editor

Shelly Harris
Contributing Editor

Tim Pollard
Jeff Land
Bekah Stoneking
Karen Jones
Delanee Williams
Bill Emeott
Kayla Stevens
Writers

Sara Lansford
Production Editor

Stephanie Salvatore
Graphic Designer

ISBN: 9781615079469
Item 005803051

DEWEY: J248.82
SUBHD: CHILDREN--RELIGIOUS LIFE \ DISCIPLESHIP \
REGENERATION (CHRISTIANITY)

Printed in the United States of America.

Kids Ministry Publishing
Lifeway Church Resources
200 Powell Place, Suite 100
Brentwood, Tennessee 37027

We believe the Bible has God for its author; salvation for
its end; and truth, without any mixture of error, for its
matter and that all Scripture is totally true and trustworthy.
To review Lifeway's doctrinal guideline, please visit
www.lifeway.com/doctrinalguideline.

All Scripture quotations are taken from the Christian Standard
Bible®, Copyright © 2017 by Holman Bible Publishers. Used by
permission. Christian Standard Bible® and CSB® are federally
registered trademarks of Holman Bible Publishers.

CONTENTS

THE GOSPEL:
God's Plan for Me

The word *gospel* means "good news." It is the message about Christ, the kingdom of God, and salvation.

 GOD RULES. The Bible tells us God created everything, including you and me, and He is in charge of everything. Invite a volunteer to recite Genesis 1:1 from memory or read it from his Bible. Read Revelation 4:11 and Colossians 1:16-17.

 WE SINNED. Since the time of Adam and Eve, everyone has chosen to disobey God (Romans 3:23). The Bible calls this sin. Because God is holy, God cannot be around sin. Sin separates us from God and deserves God's punishment of death (Romans 6:23).

 GOD PROVIDED. Read John 3:16 aloud. God sent His Son, Jesus, the perfect solution to our sin problem, to rescue us from the punishment we deserve. It's something we, as sinners, could never earn on our own. Jesus alone saves us. Read Ephesians 2:8-9.

 JESUS GIVES. Jesus lived a perfect life, died on the cross for our sins, and rose again. Because Jesus gave up His life for us, we can be welcomed into God's family for eternity. This is the best gift ever! Read Romans 5:8; 2 Corinthians 5:21; or 1 Peter 3:18.

 WE RESPOND. We can respond to Jesus. "The ABCs of Becoming a Christian" is a simple tool that helps us remember how to respond when prompted by the Holy Spirit to the gift Jesus offers.

ADMIT to God that you are a sinner. The first people God created chose to sin and disobey God. Ever since then, all people have chosen to sin and disobey (Romans 3:23). Tell God you messed up and you are sorry for doing your own thing and turning away from Him through your thoughts, words, and actions. Repent, turn away from your sin. (Acts 3:19; 1 John 1:9) Repent doesn't just mean turning from doing bad things to doing good things. It means turning from sin and even from your own good works and turning to Jesus, trusting only in Him to save you.

BELIEVE that Jesus is God's Son and receive God's gift of forgiveness from sin. You must believe that only Jesus can save you and you cannot save yourself from your sin problem—not even by praying to God, going to church, or reading your Bible. Your faith or your trust is only in Jesus and what He did for you through His life, death, and resurrection. (Acts 16:31; Acts 4:12; John 14:6; Ephesians 2:8-9)

CONFESS your faith in Jesus Christ as Savior and Lord. Tell God and tell others what you believe. If Jesus is your Savior, you are trusting only in Him to save you. Jesus is also Lord, which means He is in charge and calling the shots in your life. You can start following Him and doing what He says in the Bible. You are born again into a new life and look forward to being with God forever. (Romans 10:9-10,13)

4

FOR PARENTS

What an exciting time in your life and the life of your child. There is nothing more important than your child trusting in Jesus and having a relationship with Him. There is also no greater joy for you as a parent than the privilege of discipling your child in his faith. This book will guide you as you help your child understand what it means to be a follower of Jesus and how to trust Jesus as his or her Savior.

Use this book each week. Set aside time to complete the chapter introduction together. Then, encourage your child as she completes each daily devotion page with you or on her own.

Through this resource, you will help your child grow in his faith and learn more about God, Jesus, sin, the gospel, and more. This book will help you get started.

How to use this book

- Read the parent page for each topic to help you engage with your child as they learn.

- Read each chapter introduction with your child.

- Review daily devotionals. Encourage your child not to skip a day or do more than one day at a time, but to take the time he needs to understand the information.

- Find a quiet place to study together.

- Pray, asking God to help you learn what He wants you to know as you lead your family.

Things to have when I use this book

- Bible

- Pen or pencil

FOR KIDS

Hey Friend!

I remember when I was learning about Jesus and how He died on the cross for my sins. I had questions. One of my questions was, "What do I need to pray?" I thought you needed special words or had to say a certain prayer. I did not know that I could pray and use my own words to repent of my sin and trust Jesus to be my Savior and Lord.

Maybe you have questions too. We hope we can answer some of them. But first, we have to let you in on a secret. Guess what? We will never learn everything there is to know about God. What? Why? God is so great. Our minds cannot understand or even begin to learn everything there is to know about God. We can learn something new about God every day and never run out of things to learn! That is amazing. While we cannot learn everything, God does want us to know Him. He wants us to learn about Him.

So while we will not be able to answer every question you will ever have about God and His plan for your life, we do want to help answer some of them. God wants us to know Him. He has given us His Word, the Bible, to help us understand things about Him. God wants us to know Him because He wants to have a relationship with us. Think about it. God, who created everything, wants to spend time with you and help you know more about Him.

Grab your Bible and a pen, and let's get started learning more about God and His perfect plan to rescue us from our sin. As you work through this book, talk with your parents about what you are discovering. They can help answer your questions too.

Enjoy exploring!

Helpful tips for using this book:

❋ Gather your Bible and a pen.

❋ Find a quiet place to get comfortable.

❋ Pray, asking God to help you learn what He wants you to know.

❋ Locate at least one of the listed Scripture passages in your Bible.

❋ Read the Scripture.

❋ Ask your parents or another adult for help with any words you don't know yet.

❋ Examine the day's question and answer.

❋ Complete the activity.

❋ Talk to your parents about what you learned.

❋ If you miss a day, pick back up where you stopped.

GOD

This week you will be learning about God. Before you get started, read the Scripture passages below and answer the questions.

Revelation 4:8
Holy, holy, holy, Lord God, the Almighty, who was, who is, and who is to come.

Revelation 4:11
Our Lord and God, you are worthy to receive glory and honor and power, because you have created all things, and by your will they exist and were created.

When or where have you heard about God?

What do you already know about God?

Write down a few questions you have about God.

At the end of the week, look back at this page to see if any of your questions have been answered. If you still have some unanswered questions, ask your parents to help you look in the Bible for answers.

Q WHO IS GOD?

A God has always existed. God is all-knowing, all-powerful, and all-present. God is the Creator of our world and people. He is our Redeemer and the only one true God. God is one, and He is God the Father, God the Son, and God the Holy Spirit. God wants us to know Him, so He reveals Himself to us through His Word, creation, prayer, and people. We cannot totally understand everything about God, but we can know Him and learn about Him.

RELATED SCRIPTURES: *Genesis 1:1-2; Deuteronomy 6:4; Psalm 93:2; Psalm 147:5; Matthew 28:19; Romans 1:19*

Solve the word search to discover some of the ways God is described in the Bible.

WORD BANK:
Creator
Redeemer
Father
Healer
Almighty
Lord

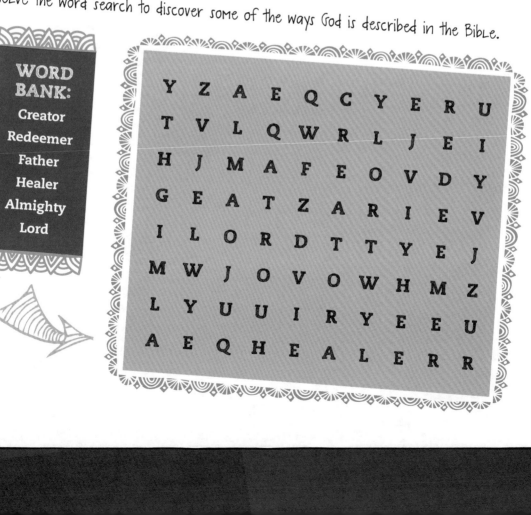

Y Z A E Q C Y E R U
T V L Q W R L J E I
H J M A F E O V D Y
G E A T Z A R I E V
I L O R D T T Y E J
M W J O V O W H M Z
L Y U U I R Y E E U
A E Q H E A L E R R

Q WHY IS GOD IN CHARGE?

A God rules over all creation because He created everything from nothing. He designed and made people, plants, animals, and more! People were created in God's image.

RELATED SCRIPTURES: *Genesis 1–2:3; Psalm 33:6; Psalm 148:5*

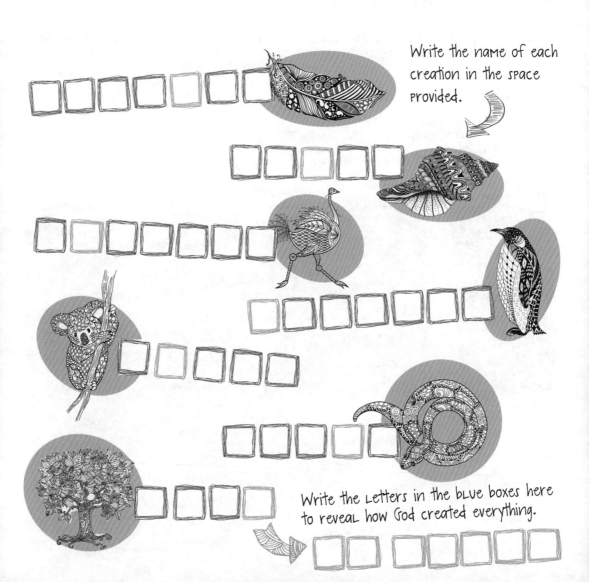

Write the name of each creation in the space provided.

Write the letters in the blue boxes here to reveal how God created everything.

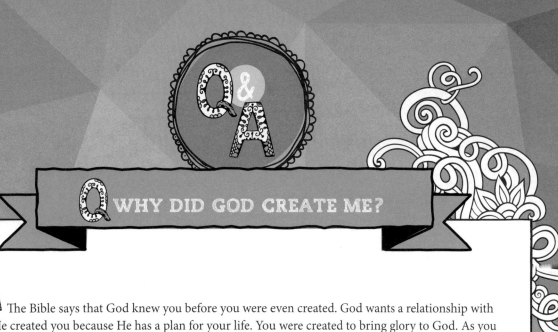

Q WHY DID GOD CREATE ME?

A The Bible says that God knew you before you were even created. God wants a relationship with you. He created you because He has a plan for your life. You were created to bring glory to God. As you grow, you will learn more about how God created you with special talents and abilities. After someone becomes a Christian, the Holy Spirit gives the person a spiritual gift. Each of your talents, abilities, and spiritual gift(s) can be used to bring glory to God.

RELATED SCRIPTURES: *Psalm 139:13-14,16; Isaiah 43:7; 1 Corinthians 10:31; 1 Corinthians 12:4-11*

ALL ABOUT ME
Fill in each blank to record some special things about you.

1 My favorite color is

2 My eyes are

3 My favorite thing to do is

4 I am good at

5 I am [   ] feet [   ] inches tall.

6 My favorite Bible verse is

7 One question I want to ask God is

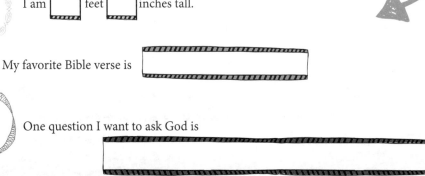

Q WHY DOES GOD PUNISH SIN?

A God is holy. He is perfectly good and righteous. God punishes sin because He is just. He always does what is right. Our sin separates us from God. Sin always has a price. The Bible tells us that the price of sin is death. Our relationship with God is broken by our sin. Created things and people get sick and die physically because sin has broken our world.

The best news is that God offers to forgive us of our sin. Jesus took the punishment for our sin when He died on the cross. We can repent of our sin and trust Jesus as our Lord and Savior.

RELATED SCRIPTURES: *Isaiah 6:3; John 3:16; John 3:36; Romans 2:5; Romans 3:26; Romans 6:23; 1 Peter 3:18*

Color all the vowels blue. Color the consonants red. What image did you discover? Why is it important?

W	C	B	Z	Q	V	R	J	C
V	G	R	J	E	Z	Q	J	Z
J	C	Q	Z	I	C	G	V	Q
B	E	U	A	O	I	O	U	C
Z	J	W	J	U	Z	B	J	W
R	U	C	V	A	V	J	I	R
E	A	E	J	E	Z	I	A	E
Q	O	G	R	U	G	C	U	J
B	O	Z	J	A	R	Q	I	G

Q WILL GOD STILL LOVE ME IF I SIN?

A God loves you, but your sin separates you from God. God knew that we could not rescue ourselves from our sin. God sent Jesus to pay the price for our sin because God loves us very much. He loves us so much that He made a way for us to be forgiven of our sin.

RELATED SCRIPTURES: *John 3:16; Romans 5:8; 1 John 4:9-10*

Hearts are used to represent the word "love." As you color the hearts, think about God's love.

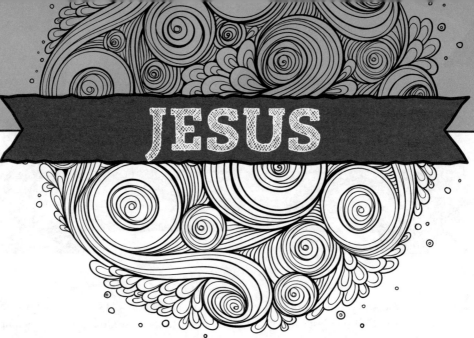

JESUS

This week you will be learning about Jesus. Before you get started, read the Scripture passage below and answer the questions.

Luke 19:10
For the Son of Man has come to seek and to save the lost.

John 1:29
The next day John saw Jesus coming toward him and said, "Look, the Lamb of God, who takes away the sin of the world!"

When or where have you heard about Jesus?

What do you already know about Jesus?

Write down a few questions you have about Jesus.

At the end of the week, look back at this page to see if any of your questions have been answered. If you still have some unanswered questions, ask your parents to help you look in the Bible for answers.

Q WHO IS JESUS?

A Jesus is God's only Son. He was born as a baby and grew as a boy. As a man, He performed miracles. He lived a sinless life. Jesus was fully God and fully human at the same time. Because Jesus loves us, He took the punishment of our sins by dying on the cross. On the third day, He arose. Following His resurrection (when Jesus came back to life), He went to be with God the Father in Heaven. He's there today and will come back to earth and take all who have received His gift of salvation (rescue from sin) to live with Him for eternity (forever).

RELATED SCRIPTURES: *Matthew 16:16; Matthew 24:36; Luke 2:10-11,52; Luke 4:16; John 3:16; Acts 1:6-11*

Use Jesus' name to make an acrostic. Write an adjective or describing word for Jesus beside each letter written below:

Q&A

Q HOW IS JESUS ALIVE?

A Jesus promised He would rise again after His death on the cross. On the third day after Jesus' death on the cross, God brought Jesus back to life. Jesus kept His promise. People saw Jesus and even touched Him. After His resurrection, He went to be with God the Father to be King over everything forever. By making Jesus alive again, God showed He accepted Jesus' death on the cross as a payment for our sins.

RELATED SCRIPTURES: *Matthew 28:1-15; John 20–21; Mark 16:1-13; Luke 24:1-49; 1 Corinthians 15:1-11*

Read Mark 16:1—13. Write or draw how you think you would have felt or what you would have said if you had seen and touched the risen Jesus.

Q WHY DID GOD SEND JESUS?

A   All people sin. Sin separates us from God and breaks our relationship with God. God loves us and wants us to have a relationship with Him. The only way people can be in relationship with Him is for someone who never sinned to die in our place. Someone needed to take our punishment. God sent His only Son to die for us. Jesus came to earth to teach about God and provide a way for us to have a relationship with God and be with Him forever. Jesus never sinned, but He died for our sins so we could have a relationship with God.

RELATED SCRIPTURES: *Matthew 1:21; Luke 19:10; John 3:16; Romans 5:8; Ephesians 2:8-9; 1 Peter 3:18*

Draw a line to match the phrase on the left to the Bible verse on the right.

GOD'S GIFT

JOHN 3:16

GOD LOVED US AND SENT HIS SON

ROMANS 5:8

JESUS DIED FOR US

EPHESIANS 2:8-9

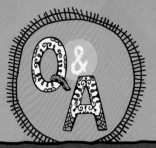

Q WHY DID JESUS HAVE TO DIE ON THE CROSS?

A God is perfect, loves every person, and wants to have a relationship with us. Our sin separates us from God. A perfect sacrifice (an offering given to God to show our need for forgiveness) was needed to take the punishment of our sins. Jesus, God's only Son, was the perfect sacrifice we needed for us to have a relationship with God and be with Him forever. Jesus willingly died on the cross because He loves us so much. He took our punishment and made the payment for our sin.

RELATED SCRIPTURES: *Luke 19:10; Romans 3:23; Romans 6:23; Ephesians 2:8-9; Philippians 2:8; 2 Corinthians 5:21*

Use the words in the word bank to fill in the blanks in the Bible verse.

WORD BANK:
God
all
glory
sinned

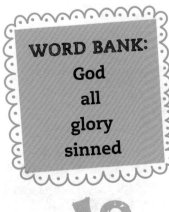

FOR _____

HAVE _____

AND FALL SHORT

OF THE _____

OF _____.

ROMANS 3:23 CSB

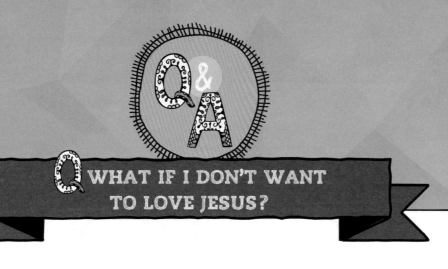

Q WHAT IF I DON'T WANT TO LOVE JESUS?

A Our sin keeps us from loving Jesus like we should. When we become a Christian, God changes our heart and we begin to love Him more. Jesus loves us regardless of if we love Him or not. He provided a way for every person to love Him and spend eternity with Him. Some people will choose not to love Him and not receive His gift of salvation. They will be separated from Him for eternity.

RELATED SCRIPTURES: *Romans 6:23; Romans 10:13; Matthew 18:14*

Think of why you love Jesus. Write a letter to Him telling Him why you love Him. If you are finding it difficult to love Jesus, write a letter to Him sharing why it's difficult to love Him.

SIN

This week you will be learning about sin. Before you get started, read the Scripture passages below and answer the questions.

Romans 3:10-11
There is no one righteous, not even one. There is no one who understands; there is no one who seeks God.

Romans 6:23
For the wages of sin is death, but the gift of God is eternal life in Christ Jesus our Lord.

When or where have you heard about sin?

What do you already know about sin?

Write down a few questions you have about sin.

At the end of the week, look back at this page to see if any of your questions have been answered. If you still have some unanswered questions, ask your parents to help you look in the Bible for answers.

Q WHAT IS SIN?

A *Sin* means "to miss the mark or standard." Sins are things that people think or do that do not line up with God's best. God gave rules for people to follow to stay in a right relationship with Him. Living by your own rules instead of living by God's rules is what we call sin. Because of sin we are separated from God, but God provided a way to restore our relationship with Him.

RELATED SCRIPTURES: *Romans 1:29-32*

HIT THE MARK
Look at the three targets below. Read the Bible verse and mark how close or far you are from obeying the verse perfectly.

Q WHO SINS?

A Everyone sins. No one who has ever lived is without sin. That means you sin, your parents sin, your teachers sin, even your pastor sins. God provided a way for people to be forgiven of their sin. Jesus is the only person ever to live on earth who did not sin. Jesus came to live perfectly by God's rules and be the way for people to be forgiven of their sin.

RELATED SCRIPTURES: *Genesis 6:12; Romans 3:10; Romans 3:23*

WHO SINS?
Find the names of people in the word search who sin. Use the word box to help you.

```
T E A C H E R
L R D E U M S
J P A S T O R
M S D T H M Y
S I B L I N G
```

Mom
Dad
Sibling
Teacher
Pastor
Me

Q WHY DO I SIN?

A Sin exists in the world because of a choice Adam and Eve made that broke God's perfect creation. Eve chose to eat the fruit of a tree God had instructed not to be eaten. Adam ate the fruit too! Because sin entered the world, all people are born sinners. People today sin when they choose something that is not God's best. We sin when we choose what we want instead of respecting God for Who He is as ruler of our lives.

RELATED SCRIPTURES: *Genesis 3:6; Romans 3:18*

WHICH FRUIT?
Circle the fruits on the tree that are good choices. Draw an X mark through the fruits that are sinful choices.

OBEYING

PLAYING NICE

HELPING

LYING

PRAYING

HITTING

 Q WHY DOES MY SIN SEPARATE ME FROM GOD?

A God is holy and cannot be in the presence of sin. The word holy means "set apart" or "separate." God's holiness means that He is perfect in every way. His perfectness makes Him separate from people. God wants Christians to be holy like Him. To be holy like God, we would need to be perfect. Since we are not—and cannot be—perfect, God sent Jesus to die for our sins so we no longer have to be separated from God. We call this justification. Justification through faith in Jesus Christ allows us to not be separated from God.

RELATED SCRIPTURES: *Isaiah 59:2; Galatians 2:16,20*

WHAT IT MEANS MATCH UP
Match the shapes below to remember five important words about your relationship with God.

SIN

REPENT

HOLY

JUSTIFICATION

FORGIVE

to turn from choosing our own way to obeying God ⬤

to be made right with God through faith in Jesus ★

to refuse to punish ✚

to be set apart or separate ◼

to miss the mark or standard ▲

 24

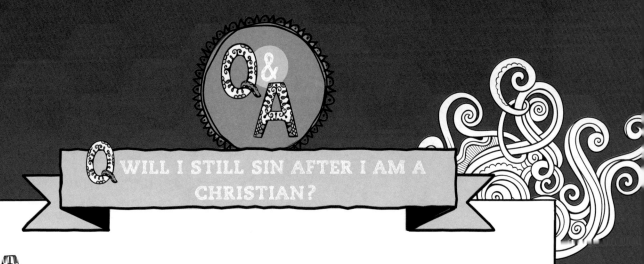

Q WILL I STILL SIN AFTER I AM A CHRISTIAN?

A Unfortunately, yes. Remember, everyone sins, and that doesn't stop after you are a Christian. The difference is, when you are a Christian and you choose your way instead of God's way, God has already forgiven you because of your faith in Jesus Christ. Studying God's Word and being with other Christians can help us make better choices about serving God, but we will still sin. The good news is, if we are sorry for our sin, and seek His help, God will help us resist any temptation (desire) to sin.

RELATED SCRIPTURES: *Romans 3:23; 1 John 1:9*

BEST CHOICES
Use your Bible to find the following verses. Write what choice you think God wants you to make in the space provided. See if you can find other things in Scripture that can be good choices.

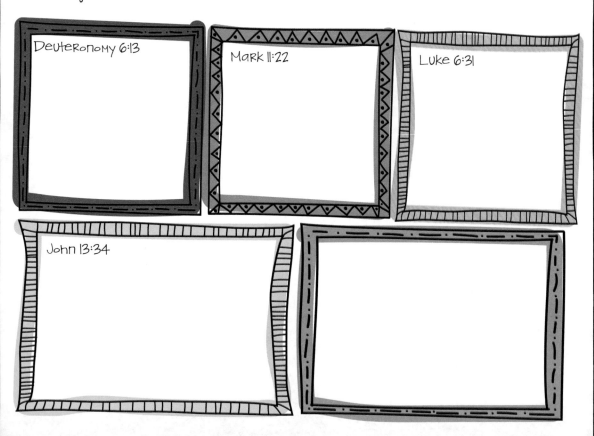

Deuteronomy 6:13

Mark 11:22

Luke 6:31

John 13:34

THE GOSPEL

This week you will be learning about the gospel. Before you get started, read the Scripture passages below and answer the questions.

John 3:36
The one who believes in the Son has eternal life, but the one who rejects the Son will not see life; instead, the wrath of God remains on him.

1 Peter 3:18
For Christ also suffered for sins once for all, the righteous for the unrighteous, that he might bring you to God. He was put to death in the flesh but made alive by the Spirit.

When or where have you heard about the gospel?

What do you already know about the gospel?

Write down a few questions you have about the gospel.

At the end of the week, look back at this page to see if any of your questions have been answered. If you still have some unanswered questions, ask your parents to help you look in the Bible for answers.

Q WHAT IS THE GOSPEL?

 The gospel is God's good news. God created everything. A special part of God's creation is people. God created people to know, love, and worship Him forever. Sadly, people choose to disobey God. This is called sin. Sin breaks our relationship with God. We can do nothing to fix this brokenness. But God, because of His great love for us, sent His Son, Jesus, to rescue us from sin. Jesus lived a perfect life, died on the cross as a punishment for our sin, then rose to life again. Only Jesus can save us. When we turn from our sin and trust Jesus as Lord and Savior, we receive God's free gift of salvation. Jesus makes us new and gives us the hope of living forever with God, and that is very good news!

RELATED SCRIPTURES: *John 1:12; John 3:16; Romans 3:23-26; Romans 5:8; Ephesians 2:8-9; 2 Corinthians 5:21; 1 Peter 3:18*

Use The Gospel: God's Plan for Me chart on page 64 to help you fill in each blank with the two words that explain each symbol.

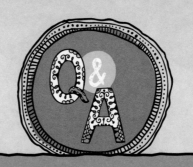

Q&A

Q WHAT IS REPENTANCE?

A *Repentance* means "to turn away" from sin—and even to turn away from doing good things to try to make up for your sin. When you repent, you turn away from (stop) doing things your own way and follow Jesus' way instead. Confessing your sin and turning away from it daily are part of what it means to be a Christian.

RELATED SCRIPTURES: *Matthew 3:8; Acts 2:38; Acts 26:20; 2 Corinthians 7:9-10; James 1:22*

Have you ever gotten dirty while playing outside? If so, you know that after you come inside, you put your dirty clothes in the laundry and you put on clean clothes. This action might help you think about repentance—when you stop sinning and start obeying God.

In the columns below, some sinful behaviors are on the left and some Christ-like behaviors are on the right. Draw a line connecting the sinful behavior to the repentant behavior you should put on instead.

TELL A LIE
GET REVENGE
THROW A FIT
ONLY THINK OF YOURSELF
TAKE THINGS YOU WANT
GRUMBLE
YELL AT YOUR MOM
HOLD A GRUDGE
BE PRIDEFUL
BE STINGY
IGNORE YOUR NEIGHBOR
DISOBEY GOD'S WORD
BE JEALOUS

DO NOT STEAL
KEEP GOD'S COMMANDS
BE THANKFUL
OBEY YOUR PARENTS
FORGIVE OTHERS
BE GENEROUS
LOVE YOUR NEIGHBOR
TELL THE TRUTH
LOVE YOUR ENEMIES
BE HUMBLE
BE JOYFUL
PRACTICE SELF—CONTROL
THINK OF OTHERS FIRST

Q&A

A Faith is believing that what God said is true. Having faith means trusting God, even if we cannot see or understand everything He says. For example, when God promised that Abraham would be the father of many nations, Abraham was old and he had no children. Abraham didn't understand how God would keep His promise, but Abraham trusted God anyway. It may not make sense that all a person has to do to be saved is to repent of her sins and trust in Jesus, but it's true! God's Word teaches that people are saved by grace through faith.

RELATED SCRIPTURES: *Genesis 15:6; Psalm 62:5-8; Romans 5:1-5; Galatians 5:22-23; Ephesians 2:8-9; Hebrews 11:1*

Follow the directions to reveal the rest of the message.

1) Cross out every Y.
2) Cross out every number.
3) Cross out every question mark.
4) Write the letters that are remaining on the blank lines to discover something else about faith.

FAITH IS A . . . _____ ____ ____ ____ _____

_____ ___ ____ ____ ____

? Y 1 F R 2 ? Y Y U 3
I ? Y T O ? 4 Y Y ? F Y T
5 H ? Y Y E S 4 ? Y P
Y ? 3 Y I ? 2 Y 1 R Y ?
2 Y I Y 3 ? T Y

Talk with a parent and pray together that God will give you faith.

29

Q WHY CAN'T I BE GOOD ENOUGH TO GO TO HEAVEN?

A Do you know anyone who is perfect like Jesus? Are you perfect like Jesus? The Bible teaches that everyone has sinned and fallen short of God's standards. Because of our sin, we can never be good enough to match Jesus' perfection. If this sounds discouraging, I have some good news for you: Going to heaven is not about what you do. Going to heaven is about what has been done for you through Jesus! This is the good news of the gospel! Turn away from your sin, and turn away from trying to earn heaven. Trust Jesus instead.

RELATED SCRIPTURES: Proverbs 16:25; Isaiah 64:6a; Mark 10:18; John 3:16; John 14:6; Romans 3:23; Romans 11:6; Ephesians 2:1-10

Unscramble the underlined words to learn something true about Jesus. Turn to John 14:6 in your Bible if you need help.

"JESUS TOLD HIM, 'I AM THE

AYW, THE RTTHU, AND THE EFIL.

NO ONE COMES TO THE AHRFTE

EXCEPT THROUGH EM.'"

✔ **EXTRA CREDIT:**
Find 3 Christians this week and ask them to share their testimonies (the stories of when they trusted in Jesus) with you.

Q WHAT AM I SAVED FROM?

A The price of sin is death. That is very serious. But the moment I put my faith in Jesus, I was justified and set free! This means God declared me "not guilty." Because Jesus paid the price for my sin, I have been saved from the punishment sin deserves. Christians are also saved from sin's control. Being saved from sin's control means being set free to love God, love others, and grow to live more like Jesus lived. This growth is called *sanctification*, and is part of the Holy Spirit's ongoing work throughout a Christian's life.

RELATED SCRIPTURES: John 3:36; Romans 3:27-28; Romans 5:9; Romans 6:6,23; Romans 8:9; Galatians 2:20; Galatians 5:1; 2 Corinthians 5:17

Write or draw pictures to show what we are set free from (Romans 8:1–2) and set free to (Mark 12:30–31) when we receive God's gift of salvation.

SET FREE FROM

SET FREE TO

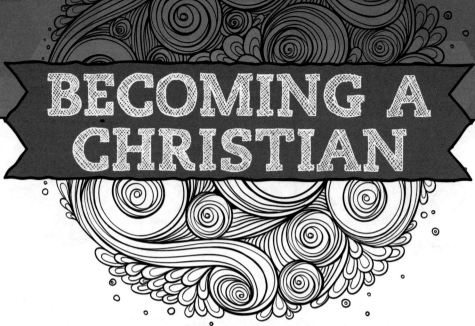

BECOMING A CHRISTIAN

This week you will be learning about becoming a Christian. Before you get started, read the Scripture passages below and answer the questions.

Romans 10:9-10,13
If you confess with your mouth, "Jesus is Lord," and believe in your heart that God raised him from the dead, you will be saved. One believes with the heart, resulting in righteousness, and one confesses with the mouth, resulting in salvation…For everyone who calls on the name of the Lord will be saved.

Ephesians 2:8-9
For you are saved by grace through faith, and this is not from yourselves; it is God's gift—not from works, so that no one can boast.

When or where have you heard about becoming a Christian?

What do you already know about becoming a Christian?

Write down a few questions you have about becoming a Christian.

At the end of the week, look back at this page to see if any of your questions have been answered. If you still have some unanswered questions, ask your parents to help you look in the Bible for answers.

Q WHAT IS A CHRISTIAN?

A A Christian is the name given to someone who has received Jesus as Lord and Savior by placing his faith in Jesus and the salvation Jesus gives through His death, burial, and resurrection. Christians are not perfect (like Jesus was) but strive to be more like Jesus each day by following His examples and teachings as shared in the Bible.

RELATED SCRIPTURES: *Acts 11:26b; Acts 16:30-31; Ephesians 5:1-2*

Use the instructions to find the answer:

CHRISTIANS FOLLOW JESUS'...

☐ The second vowel in the alphabet

☐ The third letter from the end of the alphabet

☐ The letter before B

☐ The letter after L

☐ The letter that follows the fourth vowel in the alphabet

☐ The letter that is before M

☐ The fifth letter in the alphabet

A B C D E F G H I J K L M N O P Q R S T U V W X Y Z

Q&A

Q HOW OLD DO I HAVE TO BE TO BECOME A CHRISTIAN?

A The Bible does not say how old one must be in order to become a Christian. However, there are some things a person must understand in order to trust Jesus as Savior and Lord. A person must understand his sin against God. He needs to believe that his sin against God is a big problem, but that God wants to forgive him when he asks for forgiveness. He must have an understanding of the gospel and receive God's gift of forgiveness for his sins through Jesus' death on the cross.

RELATED SCRIPTURES: *Romans 3:23-24; Acts 3:19*

Follow each letter's path and write them in the circles to find out who has sinned and who can be saved:

R E Y O E V N E

Q IF I LOVE JESUS, AM I A CHRISTIAN?

A Because of what God has done for us through His Son Jesus, our response is love. Christians certainly love Jesus, but there's more to being a Christian than just love. The Bible teaches that one must respond to the gospel, the good news of God's love. Christians have admitted to God that they have sinned and repented (turned away) from their sins. They have believed that Jesus is who He said He was—the only way to a right relationship with God and eternal life. The Bible also teaches that Christians have confessed Jesus as Savior and Lord.

RELATED SCRIPTURES: *Romans 3:23; John 14:6; Romans 10:9-10,13*

Use the grid below to identify the ABCs of becoming a Christian. Start in the center ⊚ each time:

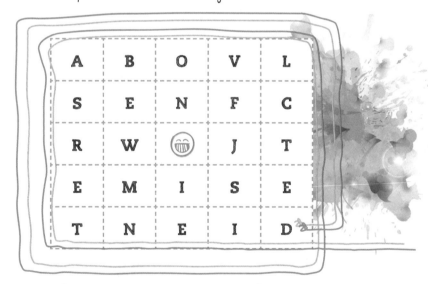

⊚ ... ↑2 ← 2 ____
⊚ ... → 2 ↓2 ____
⊚ ... ↓1 ← 1 ____
⊚ ... ↓2 → 1 ____
⊚ ... ← 2 ↓2 ____

⊚ ... ↑2 ← 1 ____
⊚ ... ↑1 ← 1 ____
⊚ ... → 2 ↑2 ____
⊚ ... → 1 ↓2 ____
⊚ ... → 2 ↓1 ____
⊚ ... → 1 ↑2 ____
⊚ ... → 2 ↓1 ____

⊚ ... → 2 ↑1 ____
⊚ ... ↑2 → 0 ____
⊚ ... ← 1 ↓2 ____
⊚ ... → 1 ↑1 ____
⊚ ... ← 1 ↑1 ____
⊚ ... ← 2 ↑1 ____
⊚ ... ↓1 → 1 ____

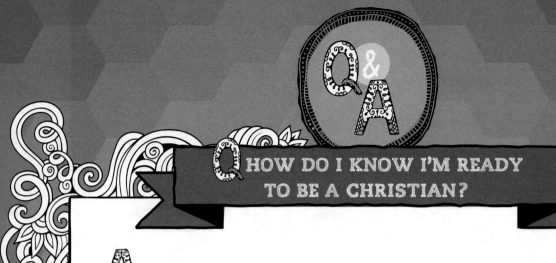

Q HOW DO I KNOW I'M READY TO BE A CHRISTIAN?

A You will never completely know and understand all the things related to salvation. No one understands all the wonders of being saved. However, you will come to know and understand what is necessary for you to become a Christian. This understanding will come as you read and study the Bible. You will learn as you listen to your pastor, Bible study teachers, and your parents. You will understand more as you ask questions and pray. Finally, God's Holy Spirit will speak to your mind and heart and help you know when it's time.

RELATED SCRIPTURES: *Romans 8:26-27; John 16:7-8*

Look at the pictures and write the first letter of each word in the blank above to discover who will help you know when it's time to become a Christian:

_____ _____ _____

____ ____ ____ ____

____ ____ ____ ____ ____ ____

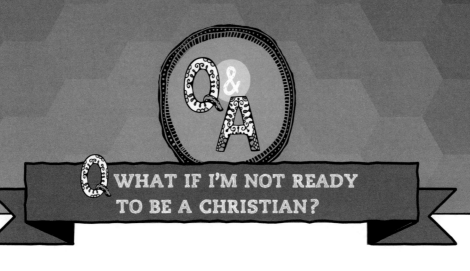

Q WHAT IF I'M NOT READY TO BE A CHRISTIAN?

A Trusting Jesus as your Savior and Lord is very personal. No one can trust Jesus for you. No one should tell you when to trust Jesus. This is between you and God. Christian adults can help you better understand about salvation, but they cannot trust Jesus for you. Nor should you make decisions about salvation just to please another person. Trusting Jesus and becoming a Christian should come when you know that God is speaking to you in your mind and heart through His Holy Spirit. God loves you very much and has a plan for your life. He will help you to respond and trust Jesus as your Savior and Lord at the right time.

RELATED SCRIPTURES: *Psalm 139:13-16; 1 Corinthians 2:10,12*

Decode the message below by replacing each letter with the letter that comes before it in the alphabet:

HPE IBT B QMBO
GPS ZPVS MJGF.

_ _ _   _ _ _   _   _ _ _ _

_ _ _   _ _ _ _   _ _ _ _ .

A B C D E F G H I J K L M N O P Q R S T U V W X Y Z

HEAVEN

This week you will be learning about heaven. Before you get started, read the Scripture passage below and answer the questions.

Revelation 21:1-3
Then I saw a new heaven and a new earth; for the first heaven and the first earth had passed away, and the sea was no more. I also saw the holy city, the new Jerusalem, coming down out of heaven from God, prepared like a bride adorned for her husband. Then I heard a loud voice from the throne: Look, God's dwelling is with humanity, and he will live with them. They will be his peoples, and God himself will be with them and will be their God.

When or where have you heard about heaven?

What do you already know about heaven?

Write down a few questions you have about heaven.

At the end of the week, look back at this page to see if any of your questions have been answered. If you still have some unanswered questions, ask your parents to help you look in the Bible for answers.

Q&A

Q WHAT IS HEAVEN?

A Heaven is God's home and where His heavenly creatures live. Heaven is a real place. Many people believe when we die, we go to live in heaven forever, but God actually has something even better for us. One day, God will make a new heaven and a new earth. We will live on the new earth forever. It will be better than we can imagine. The new earth will have everything we love about earth now but way better. Sadness, sin, and death will not be on the new earth. The best part about the new earth is that God will be there! We will live with Him and enjoy Him forever.

RELATED SCRIPTURES: *Genesis 1:1; Psalm 11:4; Isaiah 65:17; Isaiah 66:1; John 14:2-3; 2 Peter 3:13; Revelation 21:1-3*

Cross out the things listed below that will not be on the new earth. You can use your Bible to read Revelation 21:4 for help.

DEATH GOD
PAIN CRYING
JESUS SIN
JOY SADNESS
THRONE

HOW DO I GET TO HEAVEN?

A Many people believe that if they are good, they will go to heaven when they die, but the Bible teaches that none of us is good enough to get to heaven. We are sinners. Does that mean no one gets to go to heaven? No! God loves us. He wants us to live with Him forever. God sent Jesus to earth to take the punishment for our sin. When we confess our sin, turn away from it, and follow Jesus, God forgives our sin and makes us righteous (right with God). If you have trusted in Jesus, when you die, you will go to heaven.

RELATED SCRIPTURES: *Romans 3:9-12,23; Ephesians 6:23; Ephesians 2:8-9; John 3:16; 1 John 1:8-9*

How can we get to heaven? Use the key to discover the answer.

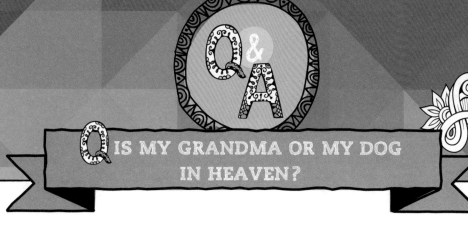

Q IS MY GRANDMA OR MY DOG IN HEAVEN?

A If your grandma trusted in Jesus to save her from sin before she died, she is in heaven with God. All people who trust in Jesus to save them from sin go to heaven when they die. Your dog never sinned. He did not need a Savior like your grandma did, but will he be in heaven? The Bible teaches that God plans to restore—or make new—everything He created that has been broken by sin. God created animals. The Bible says that animals will be on the new earth, but the Bible doesn't tell us if our pets will be some of those animals.

RELATED SCRIPTURES: *Isaiah 11:6-9; Romans 8:21-23; Romans 10:9,13; Revelation 5:13; Revelation 21:5*

Draw a picture of people and animals you hope to see on the new earth.

Q HOW DO I KNOW IF SOMEONE IS IN HEAVEN?

A We live on the earth. We cannot see heaven, so all we can know about heaven is what the Bible tells us. The Bible tells us that anyone who has turned from his sin and followed Jesus will be with Him in heaven. You may know someone who rejected Jesus his entire life, but you cannot know what was going on in his heart just before he died. He may have turned to Jesus and is with God in heaven now. We can see evidence from a person's life whether he loved God or not, but only God truly knows his heart.

RELATED SCRIPTURES: *Deuteronomy 29:29; Luke 23:40-43; Romans 10:9-10*

Unscramble the letters to reveal where a person who has trusted in Jesus to save them from sin goes when they die.

_____ _____ _____ _____ _____ _____

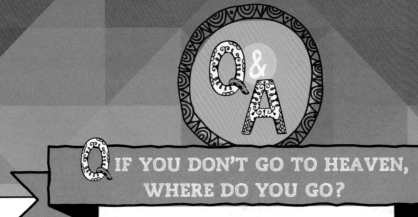

Q IF YOU DON'T GO TO HEAVEN, WHERE DO YOU GO?

A People who reject Jesus go to a place called hell when they die. Like heaven, hell is a real place, but it is not a happy place like heaven. Hell is where people are punished for their sin forever. God is holy. He will not leave sin unpunished. This is scary and sad, but that is why Jesus taking the punishment for our sin is the best news ever. God made a way so no one has to go to hell. When we put our trust in Jesus, we do not have to be afraid of hell because we know we will spend forever with God on the new earth. While we are still on earth, we should tell everyone the good news about Jesus so they can join us on the new earth.

RELATED SCRIPTURES: *John 5:23; John 15:23; Romans 1:18-20; Romans 2:5-8; 1 Thessalonians 5:9; Hebrews 9:27; 2 Peter 3:9*

List some people you know who need to hear the good news about Jesus. Pray for them. Tell them the good news about Jesus.

I WILL PRAY FOR...

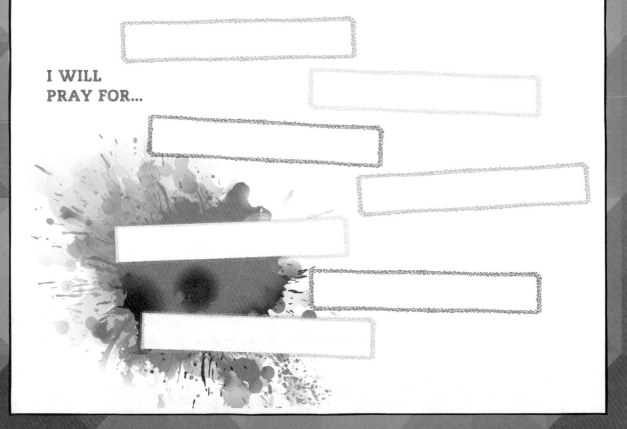

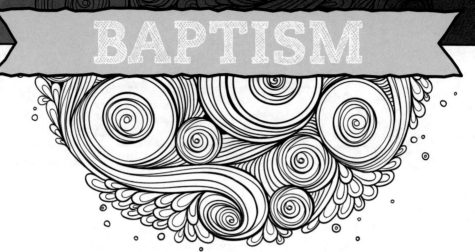

BAPTISM

This week you will be learning about baptism. Before you get started, read the Scripture passage below and answer the questions.

Matthew 3:13-17
Then Jesus came from Galilee to John at the Jordan, to be baptized by him. But John tried to stop him, saying, "I need to be baptized by you, and yet you come to me?"

Jesus answered him, "Allow it for now, because this is the way for us to fulfill all righteousness." Then John allowed him to be baptized.

When Jesus was baptized, he went up immediately from the water. The heavens suddenly opened for him, and he saw the Spirit of God descending like a dove and coming down on him. And a voice from heaven said: "This is my beloved Son, with whom I am well-pleased."

When or where have you heard about baptism?

What do you already know about baptism?

Write down a few questions you have about baptism.

At the end of the week, look back at this page to see if any of your questions have been answered. If you still have some unanswered questions, ask your parents to help you look in the Bible for answers.

Q & A

Q WHY DO PEOPLE GET BAPTIZED?

 People get baptized to obey Jesus' command and follow His example. Baptism is a one-time public act of being put under water and brought back up. This act tells others in the church that you have become a Christian. It is a picture of Jesus' death, burial, and resurrection.

Baptism was a big deal to Jesus! Since Jesus was raised from the dead once, we follow Him once in baptism. When people get baptized, they are publicly telling others in the church that they have believed in Jesus as their Lord and Savior and have chosen to follow Him. Once someone gets baptized, he usually is a member of the local church.

RELATED SCRIPTURES: *Matthew 28:18-20; Matthew 3:13-17; Romans 6:3-4; 1 Corinthians 12:12-13*

Decode the sentence to finish the message about baptism.

Baptism is a picture of Jesus'...

4   5   1   20   8,   2   21   18   9   1   12,

1   14   4

18   5   19   21   18   18   5   3   20   9   15   14.

A=1 B=2 C=3 D=4 E=5 F=6 G=7 H=8 I=9 J=10 K=11 L=12 M=13 N=14
O=15 P=16 Q=17 R=18 S=19 T=20 U=21 V=22 W=23 X=24 Y=25 Z=26

Q IF I GET BAPTIZED, DOES THAT MAKE ME A CHRISTIAN?

A Baptism does not make someone a Christian. It is your faith in Jesus that saves you. Baptism is an outward picture to others of what Jesus has already done in your life. When you decide to get baptized, it is because you have trusted Jesus to save you, and you are obeying His command to be baptized. Baptism is an opportunity to share with other Christians that God has changed your life and that you have trusted Jesus as your Savior and Lord.

RELATED SCRIPTURES: *1 Peter 3:21; Galatians 3:27; Colossians 2:12*

Solve the maze to discover the journey many people take when they are thinking about being baptized.

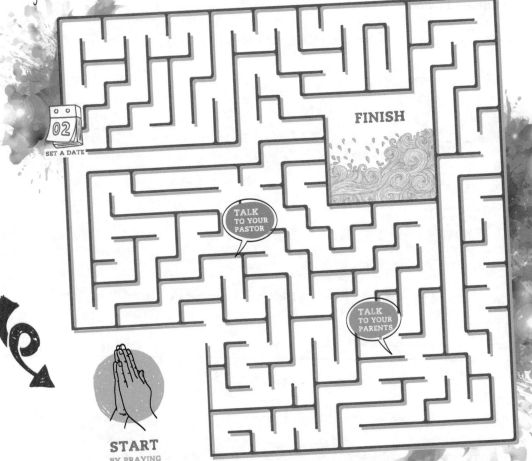

Q WHEN CAN I GET BAPTIZED?

A Baptism is for anyone who has trusted in Jesus as her Savior and is ready to become a member of the church. Baptism is for those who can share their story or testimony with others and tell what it means to trust in Jesus for salvation. The Bible does not give an exact age of how old you need to be to be baptized. It is wise to pray and talk to your family and church leaders or pastor and decide if you are ready to be baptized.

RELATED SCRIPTURES: Acts 16:31-34; Acts 8:35-38

Use the word bank to fill in the missing words from the verse. You can also use your Bible for help.

THEY SAID, "_____

IN THE _____ JESUS,

AND _____ WILL BE

_____

YOU AND YOUR _____ "

ACTS 16:31

WORD BANK:
YOU
HOUSEHOLD
LORD
SAVED
BELIEVE

Q WHAT IF I'M AFRAID OF WATER?

A You may be nervous to get baptized, especially if you are afraid of going under the water. That's OK. Being a follower of Jesus does not mean all of your fears go away. It does mean that you have trusted Jesus with your life; that includes your fears. As Christians, we believe God is bigger than our fears.

Pray and be honest with God about your fears. Ask your family to plan a time to visit with your pastor about where and how you will be baptized. He will be happy to explain all of the steps of baptism. Ask if you could visit the baptistry too. When you get baptized, your pastor will be with you to make sure you are safe. The same God who saved you will also give you peace about when the right time is for you to be baptized. He wants you to trust Him and know that He is with you, no matter what.

RELATED SCRIPTURES: *Romans 15:13; Proverb 3:5-6; Psalm 56:3*

Identify each task that involves water. Then take the circled letter from each task and unscramble it to complete the secret message.

taking a __ __ __ __

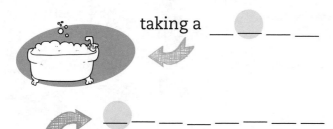

drinking __ __ __ __ __

__ __ __ __ __ __ __

pool

watering __ __ __ __ __ __ __

washing the __ __ __

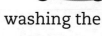

We can trust God with our

⬤ ⬤ ⬤ ⬤ ⬤ .

Q&A

A One of the first steps of your new life in Christ is obeying God's command to be baptized. Baptism is a great blessing and part of God's good plan for your life as a Christian. It is an important step in your walk with Jesus and one that you will treasure as you get older. If you feel like you are not ready to be baptized yet, talk with your parents and church leaders about your fears and concerns.

Baptism is a matter of the heart and obeying Jesus. It is a command that we want to obey because we love Jesus and have been changed by Him. Commit to pray and ask God to show you the right time for you to be baptized.

RELATED SCRIPTURES: *Ephesians 4:4-7; Romans 6:1-4*

Solve the clues to fill in the crossword puzzle using the words in the Word Bank.

WORD BANK:
baptism, water, command, blessing, Christian, obey, pray

CLUES:

1. someone who follows Jesus

2. to follow instructions or commands

3. what is used to baptize people

4. a benefit or good thing

5. how you can talk to God

6. a picture of Jesus' death, burial, and resurrection

7. an instruction to obey

THE LORD'S SUPPER

This week you will be learning about the Lord's Supper. Before you get started, read the Scripture passage below and answer the questions.

Matthew 26:26-30
As they were eating, Jesus took bread, blessed and broke it, gave it to the disciples, and said, "Take and eat it; this is my body." Then he took a cup, and after giving thanks, he gave it to them and said, "Drink from it, all of you. For this is my blood of the covenant, which is poured out for many for the forgiveness of sins. But I tell you, I will not drink from this fruit of the vine from now on until that day when I drink it new with you in my Father's kingdom." After singing a hymn, they went out to the Mount of Olives.

When or where have you heard the phrase Lord's Supper?

What do you already know about the Lord's Supper?

Write down a few questions you have about the Lord's Supper.

At the end of the week, look back at this page to see if any of your questions have been answered. If you still have some unanswered questions, ask your parents to help you look in the Bible for answers.

Q WHAT IS THE LORD'S SUPPER?

A The Lord's Supper is a time when believers remember how Jesus died on the cross to rescue them from their sin. On the night before Jesus was crucified, He celebrated the Passover with His disciples. At the Passover, Jesus took the bread and the cup and told the disciples about a new covenant. Instead of celebrating God's rescue of His people from Egypt, soon God's followers would celebrate and remember how Jesus rescued them from their sin.

RELATED SCRIPTURES: *Matthew 26:26-30; Luke 22:14-23; 1 Corinthians 11:23-29*

Circle every other letter to discover some other names used for the Lord's Supper. Start by circling the first letter of each line.

CWOLMPMQUANEIUOLNK

EAUICOHGARRCIJSBTM

_____

_____

Q&A

Q WHAT DOES THE BREAD REPRESENT?

A Jesus told the disciples that the bread represented His body. Jesus was beaten before He died on the cross. His body was bruised and injured when He was crucified. By dying on the cross, Jesus made the once-and-for-all sacrifice to atone (pay) for our sin. When we see the bread, we should remember the sacrifice Jesus made in giving His life for us.

RELATED SCRIPTURES: *Matthew 26:26; Mark 14:22; Luke 22:19; 1 Corinthians 11:23-24; Isaiah 53:5*

Jesus told the disciples to practice the Lord's Supper. Why do you think Jesus wanted His followers to remember His death on the cross? Write your thoughts in the space provided.

Q WHAT DOES THE JUICE REPRESENT?

A The juice represents Jesus' blood that He shed when He died on the cross. The juice or cup also reminds us that Jesus experienced God's wrath for our sin when He died on the cross. Jesus said the cup represented the new covenant that Jesus created when He died on the cross. In the new covenant, God would forgive and forget our sins (when we repent) because Jesus, the Lamb of God, had offered Himself as the sacrifice to pay for our sin.

RELATED SCRIPTURES: *Matthew 26:27-28; Mark 14:23-24; Luke 22:20; 1 Corinthians 11:25-26*

Solve the maze to find the grapes.

START

Q WHEN CAN I TAKE THE LORD'S SUPPER?

A The Lord's Supper is a special event. Generally people wait until after they have become a Christian to observe the Lord's Supper. This is because participating in the Lord's Supper is a way of saying that you are a follower of Jesus.

When you do participate in the Lord's Supper, it is important to do so with the right attitude. Paul told the Corinthians that believers should examine their hearts before they take the Lord's Supper. Part of examining our hearts includes realizing if we need to ask God or someone else for forgiveness. We should always do that before we participate in the Lord's Supper.

RELATED SCRIPTURES: *1 Corinthians 11:27-29*

Draw a picture of what the Lord's Supper looks like at your church.

Q&A

HOW OFTEN IS THE LORD'S SUPPER SERVED?

A Every church decides on its own how often to serve the Lord's Supper. Some churches observe it during every worship service while some choose to observe it once every few months. The Bible tells us that we should practice the Lord's Supper regularly until Jesus returns. Every time we participate in the Lord's Supper, we can look forward to a future day when we will be with Jesus forever.

RELATED SCRIPTURES: *1 Corinthians 11:27-29; Acts 2:42*

Ask your parents to help you contact your pastor or another church leader to ask a few questions about the Lord's Supper. Record the answers here.

When is the next time our church will observe the Lord's Supper?

_____

_____

How often does our church participate in the Lord's Supper?

_____

_____

Do you worry about accidentally spilling the juice?

_____

_____

What is your favorite part of the Lord's Supper?

_____

_____

_____

GOD

Trying to explain who God is to anyone is a difficult task. He is all-powerful—omnipotent, all-knowing—omniscient, and all places at all times—omnipresent. Try wrapping your head around those three things. God knows everything, can do anything, and is always around. There are so many aspects of God that one of the first things that you should explain to your child is that it is impossible for humans to understand all of who God is.

This week your child will be learning about God's power and His perfection. You child will begin to understand why God hates sin and why He cannot be around it. He will also understand that although humans sin, God's love is unconditional and there is nothing that people can do that will make Him stop loving them.

This week, as your child works through his workbook, be sure to share with him about how God has revealed Himself to you in your own life. Pray for and with your child that he will begin to see God's presence and be convicted of his sin.

The following verses will assist you as you talk to your child about who God is:

* Genesis 1:1-2
* Deuteronomy 6:4
* Psalm 139:13-14,16
* Isaiah 43:7
* John 3:16
* John 3:36
* Romans 6:23
* 1 Peter 3:18

WEEK 2

JESUS

Jesus was fully God and fully human. Understanding this concept is key to your child's understanding of how Jesus' life was the ultimate sacrifice for her sins. God sent Jesus to earth to be a man. As a man, He lived a perfect life, free of any sin and wrongdoing. He resisted temptations and taught people about who God is.

This week, help your child think about some of her sins. Help her understand that Jesus felt those same temptations, yet He never failed. Your child isn't perfect, and therefore, she needs a Savior.

As you discuss the topics for this week, encourage your child to talk about who she believes Jesus to be. Help her as she studies the reason why Jesus was the only path for forgiveness of people's sins. Your child will be challenged as she studies the topic: What if I don't want to love Jesus? Help her realize that not everyone sees the need for a Savior, but that everyone does need Jesus.

Pray for your child this week that God will open her eyes for her need for a Savior. Pray that she will become ready to receive God's precious gift of forgiveness.

The following verses will assist you as you talk to your child about who Jesus is:

- Luke 2:10-11
- Luke 2:52
- Luke 4:16
- John 20-21
- Mark 16:1-13
- Matthew 18:14
- Revelation 3:20

WEEK 3

SIN

Sin. Wow! This is a deep topic. No one really likes to discuss sin. In fact, some churches today avoid the topic altogether. Sin, however, is real and powerful. The curse of sin is death and darkness. Children are often eager to point out the sins of their siblings or friends, but they are reluctant to admit that they themselves are sinners.

Help your child understand what sin is and what sin isn't. Being tempted to sin isn't sin. Sin is when people do things that do not line up with God's best. Sin is when people do things that do not honor God.

Your child also will be challenged to be able to admit that he is a sinner as he learns that everyone sins. No one except Jesus has ever lived a life free of sin. For some children, this can be an emotional realization. Children who tend to be perfectionists, may have trouble admitting their faults.

Becoming a Christian does not mean a person will never sin again. It does mean that a person will not have to face eternal death as punishment for sin. Jesus' sacrifice paid the price. Pray that your child will seek forgiveness of his sins from Jesus.

The following verses will assist you as you talk to your child about what sin is:

* Romans 1:29-32
* Genesis 6:12
* Romans 3:10
* Isaiah 59:2
* Galatians 2:16,20
* 1 John 1:9

THE GOSPEL

The word *gospel* literally means "good news." The good news of Jesus Christ spread quickly in the early days of Christianity. People came for miles to see the Person that was said to be the Promised One. They had heard about the miracles He performed and were eager to learn from His teachings.

As the word about Jesus spread and His followers grew, there was also a growing number of people who were angry about what Jesus was teaching and doing. *As your child studies this topic of the gospel, she may question why not everyone wanted to believe in this good news.*

Help your child as she studies the word *repentance* and then seeks to understand how repentance and faith work together. The concept of faith can be difficult to explain. Try to explain to your child what faith means to you.

Your child may have friends who are from religions that are more works based. Explain to her that Christians know that faith in Jesus is the only path for salvation. A person cannot work her way to heaven, no matter how many good works she completes.

The following verses will assist you as you talk with your children about the Gospel:

- John 1:12
- Ephesians 2:1-10
- 2 Corinthians 5:21
- Acts 2:38
- Genesis 15:6
- Psalm 62:5-8
- John 3:36

WEEK 5

BECOMING A CHRISTIAN

One of the most common statements heard around churches from children is "I want to get 'babatized.'" For many kids, they equate the baptism to becoming a Christian. In reality, baptism should be more often associated with BEING a Christian. For the purpose of further clarification, you will notice in this book that the Baptism chapter does not follow this chapter.

As a parent, you have likely prayed for your child to receive Christ as his Lord and Savior. You might also feel angst in determining when your child is ready. This book is designed to help you gauge where your child is in his faith walk. Understanding your child's grasp of Jesus' sacrifice and his own willingness to accept his sin nature are key factors in a person's decision to receive Christ as his Savior.

This is a pivotal chapter and it is recommended that you work closely with your child to answer any questions that he might have. If your child decides that he wants to become a Christian at any point during this book, there is a helpful gospel plan on page 64.

One of the greatest opportunities you will have as a parent is leading your child to Christ. Some parents may be uncomfortable with this. If you would like, there are helpful videos online at *lifeway.com/kidsgospelpresentation*. Choose one of the videos and watch it with your child.

Pray that God will continue to convict your child of his need for a Savior.

The following verses will assist you as you talk to your child about becoming a Christian:

* Acts 16:30-31
* Romans 3:23-24
* Acts 3:19

* John 14:6
* Romans 10:9-10
* Romans 8:26-27

WEEK 6

HEAVEN

Probably one of the most depicted but often distorted of all religious imagery on television is heaven. Cartoons show characters floating on clouds to the pearly gates while playing harps. Some television shows depict a person who has passed away from earth now with wings and a halo. God is often depicted as a giant with a deep voice standing at a huge golden gate.

The Bible does give some ideas as to things that Christians will see in heaven, but there are still many unknowns. Christians believe that heaven is a real place. Believers look forward to the day that a new heaven and new earth will be created, and they will join Jesus for eternity.

Your child likely has many questions about heaven, and this chapter could cause more questions and maybe even some sadness. Talking about a pet's place in heaven or the probability of a loved one being in heaven can bring feelings of sadness. This chapter also discusses hell and what Christians believe about its existence. Be sensitive to your child and answer her questions honestly. Remember, however, to keep your answers age appropriate.

Pray for your child to have the desire to one day see Jesus in heaven.

The following verses will assist you as you talk to your child about what heaven is:

- 2 Peter 3:13
- Revelation 21:1-3
- Ephesians 2:8-9
- John 3:16

- Isaiah 11:6-9
- Revelation 5:13
- 2 Peter 3:9

WEEK 7

BAPTISM

Baptism is a very exciting event in the family of a child. It is a time that is often celebrated and involves family coming from out of town to witness the occasion. The fanfare is well-deserved. It is important to recognize, however, that the most amazing moment has already occurred. Your child becoming a Christian is far more important than the date of his baptism.

Despite the previous sentence, the importance of baptism should not be diminished. Jesus Himself was baptized. The Bible tells us that baptism is an outward symbol of a person's decision to follow Christ. That's just awesome!

When your child is baptized, celebrate his decision appropriately. A nice Bible or some sort of gift to commemorate the occasion is suitable. Refrain from bribing your child to make a decision to get baptized. Allow him to determine the time when he is ready to make his decision public.

As you talk to your child about baptism, remember that he might have fears of being in the public eye or maybe has fear of going under the water. You might arrange a visit to your church's baptistry to ease concerns.

Pray that the Holy Spirit will guide your child to follow Christ's example in believer's baptism.

The following verses will assist you as you talk to your child about baptism:

* Matthew 28:18-20
* Matthew 3:13-17
* Romans 6:3-4
* 1 Corinthians 12:12-13
* 1 Peter 3:21

* Galatians 3:27
* Colossians 2:12
* Matthew 14:28-31
* Romans 15:13

THE LORD'S SUPPER

Kids are fascinated with the Lord's Supper. They want to know what the cracker and the grape juice taste like. Those tiny little cups and miniature crackers make a child's curiosity grow. If your child has ever observed the Lord's Supper, he was probably full of questions: "Is that real blood?," "Is that really Jesus' body?," or "What does the juice taste like?"

The Lord's Supper is a very special time for Christians to remember Jesus' sacrifice. As you talk about the cup with your child this week, ask her why she thinks it is important to remember Jesus' blood. Talk about the bread and how it represents Jesus' body. Go over some specific behavior that a Christian should have while participating in the Lord's Supper. Remind her that it is a quiet time of reflection on Jesus' sacrifice and worship for His awesome gift.

The Lord's Supper can be a great time of conviction for a child who has made Christ her Savior. If your child hasn't made a decision yet, be sure to follow-up after Lord's Supper services and ask her if she has any questions.

In a world full of dietary restrictions, your child might be nervous to take the Lord's Supper due to gluten allergy. Consider purchasing gluten free communion bread to keep for her to be able to observe the Lord's Supper with you after she has become a Christian.

The following verses will assist you as you talk to your child about the Lord's Supper:

* Matthew 26:26-30
* Luke 22:14-23
* 1 Corinthians 11:23-29

* Mark 14:22
* Isaiah 53:5
* 1 Corinthians 11:25-26

Get the most from your study.

Customize your Bible study time with a guided experience and additional resources.

What Is a Christian? is an eight-week activity book for kids that helps them answer questions about becoming a Christian. Content covered includes questions about God, Jesus, sin, the gospel, becoming a Christian, heaven, baptism, and the Lord's Supper. An included parent section equips parents to have conversations with children who are asking questions about the gospel.

Features:

- Use with any Bible translation
- Designed for use at home with minimal supervision
- Fun activities and engaging questions that spark gospel conversations
- Great to give to kids when they are asking questions about trusting in Jesus for salvation

Lifeway designs trustworthy experiences that fuel ministry. Today, the ministries of Lifeway reach more than 160 countries around the globe. For specific information on Lifeway Kids or more product information, visit lifeway.com/iacn.

ADDITIONAL RESOURCES

I'M A CHRISTIAN NOW LEADER KIT: REVISED- 8-week study on Christian basics and discipleship for **kids** (634337883366)

I'M A CHRISTIAN NOW: YOUNGER KIDS ACTIVITY BOOK REVISED- 8-week activity book for kids activities + weekly parent pages (9781535914079)

I'M A CHRISTIAN NOW: OLDER KIDS ACTIVITY BOOK REVISED- 8-week activity book for kids activities + weekly parent pages (9781535914086)

GROWING IN MY FAITH: A 90-day devotional for kids about healthy spiritual habits (9781462740987)
Digital: (9781087731285)

THE LIFE OF JESUS: A 90-day devotional for kids about the life and ministry of Jesus (9781535935784)
Digital: (9781087731346)